Farm Machines at Work

Balers
Go to Work

Emma Carlson Berne

Lerner Publications ◆ Minneapolis

To Bruce Gaskins, for patiently explaining the finer points of farm equipment and for answering many phone calls

New Holland is a registered trademark of CNH International and is used under license.

Lerner Publications Company
A division of Lerner Publishing Group, Inc.
241 First Avenue North
Minneapolis, MN 55401 USA

For reading levels and more information, look up this title at www.lernerbooks.com.

Main body text set in Billy Infant Semibold 17/23.
Typeface provided by SparkyType.

Library of Congress Cataloging-in-Publication Data

Names: Berne, Emma Carlson, author.
Title: Balers go to work / Emma Carlson Berne.
Description: Minneapolis : Lerner Publications, 2018. | Series: Farm machines at work | Includes
    bibliographical references and index.
Identifiers: LCCN 2017054193 (print) | LCCN 2017055688 (ebook) | ISBN 9781541526051 (eb pdf) |
    ISBN 9781541526020 (lb : alk. paper) | ISBN 9781541527669 (pb : alk. paper)
Subjects: LCSH: Agricultural machinery—Juvenile literature. | Baling—Juvenile literature.
Classification: LCC S675.25 (ebook) | LCC S675.25 .B46 2018 (print) | DDC 631.3—dc23

LC record available at https://lccn.loc.gov/2017054193

Manufactured in the United States of America
1-44570-35501-3/29/2018

TABLE OF CONTENTS

FARMS
NEED BALERS

Farms need hay for animals to eat. Farmers use hay balers to gather and store the hay. The block or roll of hay is a bale.

There are two types of balers. Round balers make round bales of hay. Square balers make square bales.

Smaller farms use small square bales, while large farms with many animals to feed use big, round bales.

This machine cuts the hay.

The baler is one part of haymaking. First, hay is cut and dried. Next, it is raked. Then the farmer attaches a baler to the back of a tractor. The tractor pulls the baler through the fields.

The baler picks up the cut hay. It squeezes the hay into a bale. Then farmers put the bales in animal feeders or stack them in a barn.

Different-sized balers make different-sized bales.

2 EXPLORE
THE BALER

A rake-like tool called a pickup grabs the hay from the bottom of the baler. It pulls the hay into a space inside the baler called the bale chamber.

This drawing shows how a round baler makes hay bales.

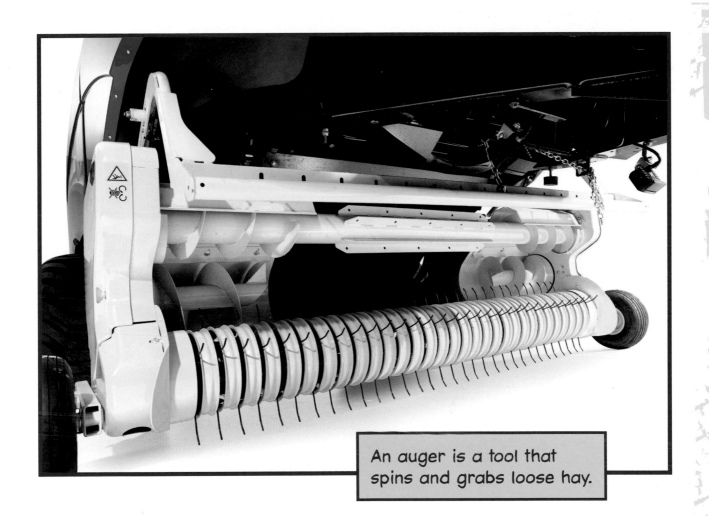

An auger is a tool that spins and grabs loose hay.

In a round baler, rubber belts and metal rollers press the hay. In a square baler, the inside of the bale chamber holds the hay in place. An auger feeds the hay into a second space inside the baler.

The plunger also cuts the ends of the hay so it forms into the correct shape.

In a round baler, the belts twirl, grabbing hay. In a square baler, a plunger packs the hay down tight.

The baler wraps twine around the bale to hold the hay in place. Then the bale gets pushed out the back of the baler and onto the ground.

Farmers use their balers whenever they make hay. Haymaking usually happens between May and August.

Farmers put round bales into feeders for animals to eat. Farmers often feed square bales to cattle in feedlots.

Special feeders hold large bales so cattle can eat easily.

Farmers often feed mini bales to horses.

Some bales are small and rectangular. These are mini bales. Mini bales are small enough for one person to lift.

In the past, farmers raked hay into haystacks. The hay wasn't baled. It was stored loose in a field or barn.

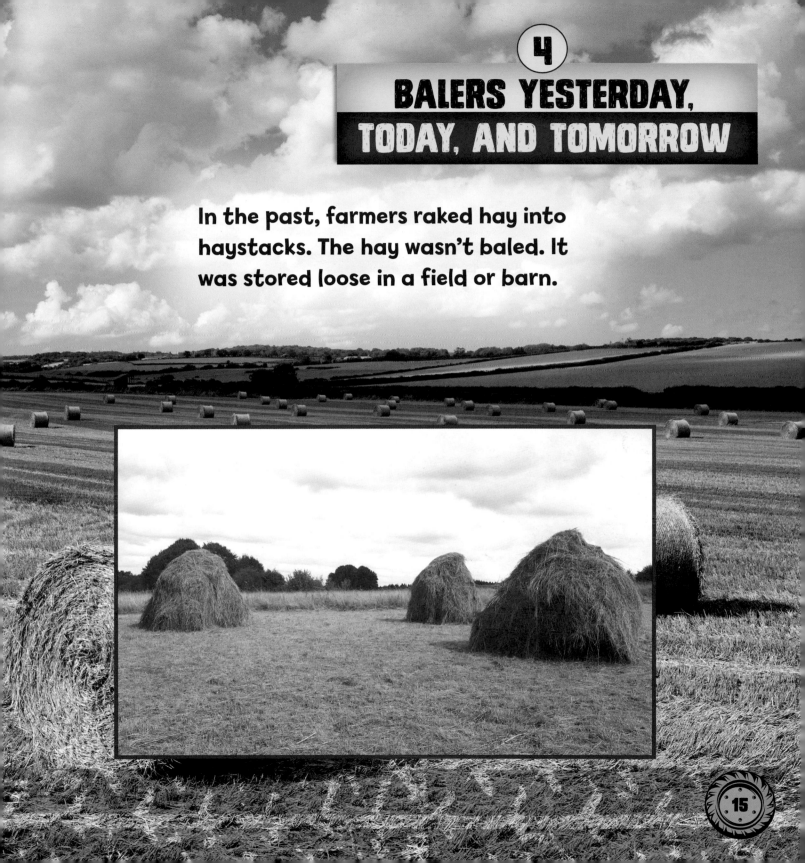

In the nineteenth century, farmers used horses to help them collect hay. The horses led carts that carried the hay. Farmers also used horse-drawn balers.

16

Workers still had to tie the bales with twine by hand.

Later, steam engines powered balers. Tractors were invented in 1892. In the 1930s, farmers began pulling balers behind their tractors.

Farm manufacturers are always working to make balers better. Computers on some modern balers can send messages to tractors. The baler tells the tractor when to slow down or speed up.

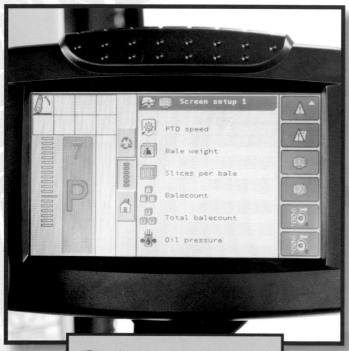

The baler also tells the tractor to stop when the bale is big enough.

Hay and balers are part of everyday life on a farm. Working with balers gets easier for farmers as technology improves.

BALER
PARTS

belts

pickup

auger

tire

FUN BALER FACTS

- If hay is not dried properly, it will rot after it is baled.

- Sometimes farmers use big, square bales to build temporary pens for sheep and other farm animals.

- One of the largest types of balers made round bales of hay 7.5 feet (2.3 m) wide and 5.5 feet (1.7 m) across!

GLOSSARY

auger: a tool inside a baler that can twirl and grab hold of hay

feedlot: a big space where cattle are kept and fed

haymaking: the steps of harvesting hay and turning it into bales to feed to animals

manufacturer: a company that makes goods for sale

plunger: a part in a machine that moves up and down, usually packing something down

twine: strong string

FURTHER READING

Balers
http://www.kidsfarm.com/equipbalers.htm

Boothroyd, Jennifer. *Tractors Go to Work*. Minneapolis: Lerner Publications, 2019.

Dittmer, Lori. *Balers*. Mankato, MN: Creative Education, 2018.

Dufek, Holly. *Busy on the Farm with Casey & Friends*. Austin, TX: Octane, 2017.

My American Farm
http://myamericanfarm.org/classroom/games

Weingarten, E. T. *Hay Balers*. New York: Gareth Stevens, 2016.

INDEX

PHOTO ACKNOWLEDGMENTS

The images in this book are used with the permission of New Holland except: Tatiana Kasyanova/Shutterstock.com, p. 1 (background); Fabio Alcini/Shutterstock.com, p. 5 (inset); David Crosbie/Shutterstock.com, pp. 8, 15 (background); © Alexandre Dulaunoy/flickr.com (CC BY-SA 2.0), p. 15 (inset); Vyntage Visuals/Shutterstock.com, p. 16; Brian A Jackson/Shutterstock.com, p. 21; Laura Westlulnd/Independent Picture Service, p. 23 (tractor). Design elements: enjoynz/DigitalVision Vectors/Getty Images; CHEMADAN/Shutterstock.com; pingebat/Shutterstock.com; LongQuattro/Shutterstock.com.

Cover: New Holland.

EXPLORE MORE

Learn even more about balers! Scan the QR code to see photos and videos of balers in action.